eBay 2021

5 Moves You Need to Make Today to Sell More Stuff on eBay

Copyright © 2021 by Nick Vulich

Table of Contents

Getting Started 1
Plan for Success 8
Find Your Niche 16
Ship Like a Pro 20
    Package Your Items Like a Pro 27
    Set Up Your Shipping Station 28
    Must-Have Supplies 30
    Packaging Tips 34
    Do I Need to Offer Free Shipping? 38
    Setting Shipping Rates in eBay 41
    Printing Shipping Labels Using eBay & PayPal 46
    Do I Need Insurance? 50
    Using a Third-Party Shipping Provider 53
Sell International 60
    eBay Global Shipping Program 63
    Enable Items for International Shipping 67
    List Your Items on International Sites 73
    Open an International eBay Store 80

 Customs Forms..82
Getting Down to Business 86
 What You Need to Know About Taxes 87
 Most Common Tax Deductions 94
 Choosing Your Business Structure 99
 Business Permits, Licenses, and Such................................103
Sell your Stuff Off eBay 106
 Sell it on Amazon..108
 Sell it on Etsy 111
 Sell it on Fiverr..115
 Sell it on Your Personal Website..120

Getting Started

It's been nearly a decade since I published my first book detailing how to sell on eBay. Since then, the marketplace has undergone many changes—some good, some not so good.

The only sure thing for online sellers is that change is inevitable. Sellers need to be quick on their feet and agile enough to execute at a moment's notice.

Looking back, the most significant change over the past decade has been the decline in auction sales. Everything now is fixed-price, with a side-order of best-offer.

Fixed price listings are great, but...

They keep you from posting items at your best price because you need to leave a little wiggle room in case the other guy wants a discount.

They prevent you from getting the most money possible. Bidding wars were the most exciting part of old-time selling. You could list an item at 99¢, expecting it might go all the way to ten bucks. The next thing you know, it hit $250 because two wild and crazy guys got caught up in a bidding war.

I miss that stuff!

Don't get me wrong. Auction listings still work, but they're not what they used to be. I can list 500 auctions this week and sell twenty items—most of them at the starting bid. Ten years ago, if I listed 500 items, I would have gotten a minimum of 100 sales. Half of them would have sold at the buy-it-now price, seventeen dollars higher than my opening bid. Most of the others would have drawn several bids. That doesn't happen today.

Is it me or eBay? That's a question you'll have to figure out for yourself.

The newest elephant in the room is eBay's managed payments. Twenty years ago, they pushed all their sellers to switch to PayPal and slam all your business through there. Five years ago, they sold PayPal.

Now that eBay's agreement with PayPal is over, they're forcing sellers into their managed payment system. Again, it's good and bad. eBay collects your money, holds it for a few days, and pays you less your seller fees. For sellers who've posted items on Amazon, getting your money in a few days is a big deal because Amazon only issues payments twice a month. For eBay sellers used to PayPal, it's a problem. PayPal let you withdraw your money literally seconds after the buyer paid.

Sellers are mad, and justifiably so.

Many are used to pulling cash out whenever they needed it—for gas, food, bubblegum, or whatever. Now, they have to wait.

Professional sellers depended on the immediate cash flow to keep their business running. Now they're jumping through hurdles to get cash when they need it. Taking out your fee as you go sounds good, but many sellers counted on that money to get them through the month. The timing is off.

If you're a high-volume seller, managed payments can save you a significant amount of money on listing fees. A premium store used to come with 1,000 no-cost fixed listings. It still does, but now eBay is offering sellers using managed payments up to 75,000 bonus listings. The exact number of zero-cost items depends upon your store level and the categories you list in. For sellers like myself, that's a significant savings.

When eBay opened the offer, I was on the verge of moving up to an anchor store for another $300 per month. The managed payments bonus listings have put another $3600 a year in my pocket, so I'm thrilled with the service.

Except...

There's no guarantee it's going to last. eBay is careful to promote them as "promotional offers" in your selling manager. The start and end date changes to the current month. That means eBay can take your no-cost listings away as quickly as they gave them. Nothing is free forever. Enjoy the extra listings while they're available.

Welcome to eBay selling. There's nothing you can do about it. It's either accept the changes or pack up and leave.

eBay doesn't care.

Really.

The other big thing is Covid-19.

Online sales are exploding—for eBayers who sell necessary items. Not so much, for everyday sellers of collectibles, books, clothes, etc. Once everyone is vaccinated and people get out and about again, things should return to normal.

Traditional retailers are counting on a newly-coined term—revenge buying. The thinking is that as the pandemic is winding down, people will emerge from hibernation and rush down the street throwing hundred dollar bills here and there. They expect to get their share of the freshly printed Biden-Bucks Some of it should come your way, too.

The pandemic has caused another problem for online sellers. Buyers want their items now, but shippers can't keep up.

The post office took up to two weeks to deliver first-class items at Christmastime. The standard delivery time is three to five business days.

As you can guess, customers got upset and demanded refunds.

Those issues hit sellers where they were already hurting—in the pocketbook.

Now the post office is looking at streamlining service—possibly making fewer or centralized deliveries and extending delivery times.

And, oh yeah, to stay solvent, they need to bump their rates again.

It's gonna tear a hole in your pocketbook.

Why am I telling you this? Because no one else will. They're afraid you won't buy their book if no one's buying anything from you. I'm not going to lie to you.

It sucks, but...

If you're already selling on eBay, odds are you're feeling the pain. If you're new to eBay, keep in mind—selling on eBay doesn't mean you aren't going to hit some rough patches now and then.

Most books that talk about selling online paint a rosy picture. They tell potential sellers that once you post your items for sale on eBay, you can spend the rest of your time lying around the house in your jammies or undies watching

TV. Money will pour into your PayPal account 24 / 7. That's the dream for surviving the Covid pandemic, isn't it?

I wish I could tell you it was so, but that'd be a bit like tossing you under the bus.

I will tell you that after you've been selling on eBay for a while, it gets easier. You'll make more sales. Many buyers will return to buy from you if you give them good value for their money and excellent customer service.

Just keep in mind—it's a roller coaster ride, no matter how long you've been selling on eBay. Sales vary by season. Usually, the summer months—June through August are the slowest time. The Christmas season—November through January is traditionally the strongest selling period. Many eBay sellers earn fifty to seventy-five percent of their profit during the holiday season. Where your sales fall on the scale depends on the type of products you sell.

Ideally, you will develop a product mix that balances your sales out so you don't experience extreme seasonal fluctuations. It won't happen magically, though. It's something you need to plan for and work into your marketing mix.

Sometimes you'll have a situation where you've been selling the same product for five or ten years. Suddenly, sales stop. The market goes dead. When this occurs, you need to assess the situation quickly and determine what happened. Did a new competitor enter the marketplace and undercut your prices? Was a new product released that makes yours obsolete? Are there too many sellers offering the same products that you are selling?

Whatever you do, you need to react quickly? Otherwise, it's like beating a dead horse. You'll never get anywhere.

Hopefully, you've got a Plan B. That's what this book is all about. How to sell on eBay today—and tomorrow. To do that successfully, you need to move from Point A to Point B without tripping over your own feet.

Nothing I'm going to teach you here is new. This book isn't going to walk you through listing your items on eBay. Plenty of other books do a great job of that.

There are no hidden secrets—no magic formulas. Selling on eBay isn't rocket science. It takes hard work and common sense. You don't need any fancy degrees. A business degree can hold you back by making you overthink things.

If you can execute in five key areas, you'll have everything you need to succeed in online selling—today, tomorrow, and into the future.

1. Plan for success
2. Establish a Niche
3. Ship like a pro
4. Sell international
5. Know your numbers

Plan for Success

Too many sellers rush into eBay without a plan.

They jump in and start selling before they understand what the market is all about. Other newbies are sloppy. They post poorly lit pictures or write vague descriptions that don't really tell buyers anything about what they're selling. Too often, sellers overprice or underprice items in their haste to get their listings posted. If they overprice their item, it doesn't sell. Then, they decide eBay doesn't work. It's just another scam. Something that stole their money. If they underprice their item, and it sells, they complain because they can't make any money.

Selling on eBay is part art and part science.

I can teach you the science or the mechanics of selling on eBay, but to be successful, you need to understand the art of selling on eBay. What I call gut instinct.

When you scout inventory, you need to walk through a room and instantly zero in on the money items.

I sell books, magazines, and paper memorabilia. At estate sales, that's all I'm looking for on my first round through the house.

I look for vintage magazines. I've got a mental list of about twenty-five titles I always buy. What really excites me is when I come across something new. Something I've never seen before. The more pictures the magazines have in them, the more I want them.

I also scan the room for items I don't typically sell. Things I think would complement my product line. Here's the way I look at it. If you see something new and unique that appeals to you, it's going to have that same effect on buyers in your niche.

Mike on American Pickers put it best, "In my business if you come across something you've never seen before, the best time to buy it is now."

If you don't have that gut instinct to recognize something good, it will be harder to succeed on eBay.

Here's why?

If you don't have that gut instinct to recognize what's good and what's not, it's going to be like walking into a room with blinders on. There may be fifty items you can double or triple your money on. However, you're likely to miss every single one of them because you're laser-focused on just a few items you're comfortable selling.

That's good for the guy behind you. He's going to grab everything you walked by. He's going to be able to pay his bills this week.

But it sucks for you.

You're going to be right back to thinking eBay is a scam. There's no way anyone's making any money on the site.

It happens every day.

Don't believe me? Just hop on any eBay forum and get a whiff of all the bitching and whining. Need some more convincing? Stop by the *Ecommerce-Bytes Blog* and check out some of the comments for any of their eBay-related articles. It's the same people—constantly whining about how horrible and mean eBay is. How they can't make a dime anymore because of that old Scrooge-like Mr. eBay.

Guess what?

It's not eBay. It's you and your stinking attitude.

The sooner you understand that whether you make or lose money on eBay is all about you and how you approach selling, the sooner you'll find the success you're looking for.

Let me tell you a story.

I was a salesman covering a four-state area (Iowa, Illinois, Missouri, and Wisconsin) for more years than I care to remember. I also sold historical memorabilia and sports cards on eBay. I popped listings up in between trips and phone calls, and I wasn't doing half bad. Most months, I made $1500 to $2000 profit, $5 to $10 at a time.

One day I received a call from the VP of sales. My position was being eliminated, but not to worry. They were offering a severance package. The company wouldn't contest my unemployment, and they'd give me a good reference. Of course, they did need one small favor in return—I had to sign a paper promising not to sue them for any of this.

What do you do?

If you want the money, you need to sign. To make a long story short, I signed the papers. I put work behind me and decided I was going to make a serious run at eBay.

If you tuned me out for reminiscing, here's where you might want to tune back in.

I decided to make a serious run at selling on eBay.

By most standards, I was already making good money. Fifteen hundred to two thousand dollars a month isn't pocket change. The thing is: If I was going to make a living selling on eBay, I needed to double or triple that number before my unemployment and severance pay ran out. That gave me roughly six months to go from so-so to oh-boy.

To do that required some serious planning.

Make a Plan

Anybody can make a few sales on eBay. The key to success is to keep those sales growing while at the same time discovering new products to sell and new avenues to make your offerings available through.

It isn't as easy as it sounds.

To be successful selling on eBay, you need to have a plan. You need to work your plan.

I was lucky. I already knew what I wanted to sell. A lot of sellers who are new to eBay stumble when they're asked that question. For many new sellers, uncertainty about what to sell is the major stumbling block that keeps them from becoming successful.

I will cover that topic in much more detail in the section about how to discover your niche. For now, were going to concentrate on some more complex questions.

Who are my customers? Why should they buy from me?

If you're already selling on eBay, it's going to be much easier to answer these questions. The best way to do this is to ask your customers directly. Every time you send out a customer service email, include a brief survey.

It can be as simple as,

Thanks again for making your purchase from history-bytes. We realize you have lots of options to choose from when purchasing historical collectibles on eBay. The fact you chose to do business with us is a great honor.

Please take a few moments to check your items over carefully when they arrive, and make sure they meet your expectations. Should you have any questions or concerns, please feel free to contact me personally. I will be happy to do whatever I can to make it right for you.

Could I also ask a small favor?

Here at history-bytes, we're always trying to make your shopping experience more enjoyable. Would you have a few moments to tell us about your experiences with history-bytes and why you chose the items you did?

It will help us accomplish two important tasks:

1. It will help us ensure a pleasant shopping experience for our customers.

2. It will help us to select more products that our customers want and need.

To make it as easy as possible, just click reply to this email and tell us what you like or don't like about shopping with history-bytes. Next, tell us why you purchased your item and how you intend to use it. Finally, tell us what other items you'd like to see us carry.

Thanks again for making your purchase from history-bytes. If you were able to make time for our survey—you're amazing. Rest assured, we'll use that info to make your shopping experience with history-bytes even better.

Have a great day!

That's all there is to it. Take our survey. Make it your own. Feel free to change it up a bit. Personalize it for your business. Ask about specific products, different parts of the shopping experience, or what customers like or don't like about your eBay store or listings.

You'll be surprised what you learn. It just may help you rocket your sales to a new level.

If you're new to eBay and don't have any customers, you will have to work things a little differently. Most of your research will analyze sales trends and use your gut instincts to determine how that data affects you.

Conduct an advanced search for items similar to yours.

If you've never run an advanced search before—don't panic. It's super easy to do. Look for the search box at the top of the eBay page. Just to the right of it, you'll see the word "advanced." Click on it.

This will take you to the advanced search page. It seems overwhelming at first, but there are only a few areas of it you need to use.

The most important thing you need to understand is the only information that counts is what you find in sold listings. Anybody can list anything they want to on eBay and ask for a crazy amount of money. We separate the wheat from the chaff and get to the good stuff by analyzing completed sales. Ones where people spent money to buy something.

This tells us the seller did something right with their listing.

Find Your Niche

Selling on eBay is a bit of a pig in a poke. You can sell pretty much anything, but you need to offer a unique line of complimentary products to make money consistently.

Sure. Some sellers make a good living selling yard sale, garage sale, and flea market finds. Most burn out quickly and give up because they can't build traction. Buyers don't come back because your products are one-off.

Suppose you find an old Polaroid camera that you bundle with a few packs of film. It sells for fifty bucks. That's good, but where's your buyer going next?

To someone else's eBay store if he's a camera fanatic. A quick search of your store shows a leather coat, some old shoes, and a hair dryer. Nothing to do with cameras, so the buyer moves on without bookmarking your store.

No more sales for you!

To consistently make money selling on eBay, you need to develop a complimentary product line and add value to it. Explain what they're for. How they're used, and why buyers should choose it over another product.

Finally, you've got to sell yourself. Tell buyers why they should purchase something from you rather than some other seller.

I'm a history fanatic who's written over fifty books dealing with early American history. I've sold over 30,000 vintage magazine articles and prints over the last twenty-one years.

If you've got a question about vintage paper, I've got an answer. My customers know it, and they keep coming back for more.

That's the kind of niche you want to develop.

It's got to be a unique product with fanatical buyers. And you need to know more about it than your customers.

Sounds hard, doesn't it?

It's not.

It just takes time and study.

What's your passion?

Baseball cards. Stamps. Coins. Wine. Old locks. Western Americana. Science. Astronomy.

People are interested in all those subjects and more. You just need to pick one that you're interested in and take a deep dive into it

Learn everything you can and incorporate some of that knowledge in each listing. Barring that, snatch the information you need off Wikipedia.

If you get another Polaroid camera, paste in some information about its development and history. Then raise your asking price a few bucks.

See what happens.

Suppose you sell used smartphones. So do thousands of other sellers.

If you want to differentiate yourself, engineer a unique shopping experience.

If they're listing an iPhone 12, most sellers will copy and paste Apple's specs into the listing. As a result, every listing is going to look alike.

What if you approached it differently?

Instead of listing the phone's features, explain what they can do for you.

Focus on the camera. Apple has a spec sheet that talks about the different camera features, but it's technical and hard to follow. Put it in terms a twelve-year-old can understand. Make it fun and tell how the camera will improve your selfies.

Target the camera to other eBay sellers. Talk up how easy it is to snap product photos and upload them into their listings.

When you target a niche market, you reach a different segment of buyers. Price is no longer the deciding factor. These customers buy based on what the product can do for them. They buy from you because you reached them. You know what you're talking about.

If you want to make more money selling on eBay, find a niche and nurture it for all it's worth.

Ship Like a Pro

Understanding how to ship the items you sell is just as important as knowing which items to sell.

Online sellers face two different shipping situations: domestic (shipping within your home country) and international (shipping outside of your home country). Many sellers spend years trying their hardest to avoid making international sales. They're afraid of the extra paperwork involved or that there may be excessive damage claims, theft, or negative feedback caused by shipping or communication glitches.

The truth is international shipping is no more complicated than domestic shipping. It's just a matter of learning and getting used to the extra paperwork involved.

Domestic Shipping

Most of the shipping you're going to do is considered domestic shipping or shipping within your home country.

The Post Office offers many different ways to ship items. The shipping method you choose depends upon the item you are shipping, its size, value, and how quickly you want it to arrive.

Here is a breakdown of the most common shipping services available from the post office and the different items you can ship with them.

- **Media mail** is designed for shipping books, CDs, DVDs, and other educational materials. Media mail does have a few restrictions. The material cannot contain any advertising pages, so most magazines are ineligible for media mail shipping.

    Packages sent by media mail are subject to inspection by the post office. If you include ineligible items, they can return your package's postage due. The main advantage to sellers from using media mail is it's cheaper to ship heavier items like books. As a result, you can offer your customers a less expensive delivery option. This is especially important if you are selling in the book category because it will keep your listing competitive

    Delivery time usually is 3 to 8 business days but can vary based on the season. At Christmas time, it can take as much as two to three weeks to deliver a media mail package, so be sure to give buyers a heads up – "Hey. It's cheap, but it's slow." That way, they understand it's the post office, not you.

Covid-19 is creating more shipping difficulties. The post office has fewer employees able to work, so shipping delays are a constant problem. Many sellers have emailed me recently to let me know they shipped my package. Still, it's likely to take longer to deliver because of the pandemic.

Warning your customers upfront of possible shipping delays can prevent problems down the line and possible negative feedback.

- **First Class**. If you ship smaller items (less than 13 oz.), first class will be the most economical method available. You can ship just about anything—books, clothes, DVDs, CDs, jewelry, stamps, postcards, you name it. The problem is tracking is not available on all first-class packages, so you cannot offer proof of delivery. If you are a top-rated seller, that's a no-no.

   If you mail flat items like baseball cards and postcards, then you cannot add tracking. Your package is required to be a minimum of 1/8" thick. Delivery time usually is 1 to 3 days depending upon where you are sending your package. Again, Covid-

19 can stretch first-class delivery times to a week or more.

- **Priority Mail**. The majority of items sold by online sellers are shipped by priority mail. It has several advantages over other services, including:

  ✓ You can mail heavier items than first class,
  ✓ Most items are delivered within 1 to 3 days.
  ✓ Tracking is available on all packages, so you have proof of delivery for eBay and your customers.
  ✓ The Post Office provides free shipping materials, so you don't have to invest in boxes and other expensive packaging materials.
  ✓ You can schedule a pickup, and the post office will send a carrier to your home or business to pick up your packages. They also do this for first-class mail, now.
  ✓ The disadvantage to using priority mail is that it is more expensive than first class or media mail.

- **Priority Mail Flat Rate** takes the guesswork out of shipping. You can ship whatever will fit in the package regardless of the weight anywhere in the United States for a preset fee. This is an excellent option for buyers and sellers because it's less expensive to ship heavier items or multiple items that fit in a single package.

Like regular priority mail—it's quick, offering 1 to 3-day delivery, comes with delivery confirmation, and packaging materials are free from the Post Office. Be sure you use the Flat Rate Priority Mail boxes when using this service.

- **Express Mail** offers overnight delivery service to most areas in the United States. If your customer needs an item quickly, this is the service for them. Be aware it's expensive, and the fees are based on the package's size and weight.

    Like Priority Mail, Express Mail offers free packaging materials and delivery confirmation. Sellers also receive $100 of insurance free with most parcels sent and signature delivery confirmation which eBay and PayPal require on more expensive packages.

- **Priority Mail Express Flat Rate** offers next-day delivery (in most areas), plus the added convenience of simplified rates. When you use the flat rate boxes, anything you mail in them (regardless of weight) ships for one fee, so if you're shipping heavy items—this is the service for you.

If you want to get the full scoop on these delivery services, check out the following link. https://www.usps.com/ship/compare-domestic-services.htm

- **eBay Standard Envelope**. Early in 2021, eBay introduced a new shipping service called eBay standard Envelope. It's a way for sports card sellers to offer low-cost tracking on items valued under $20. The cost is very reasonable—between 51 and 91 cents, compared to $ for priority shipping.

eBay Standard Envelope comes with many restrictions. You can read more here. https://pages.ebay.com/ebaystandardenvelope/index.html.

Currently, the service is off to a bumpy start. e-Commerce Bytes blog reports many sellers say tracking is nonexistent, most likely because postal employees aren't scanning the packages. Service could improve as postal employees become more aware of it. For now, beware and ship at your own risk.

For sellers in other low-value categories where tracking is not cost-effective, eBay says they are expanding the service. Let's hope they eliminate the bugs before moving forward.

Package Your Items Like a Pro

How you package the items you sell makes a significant difference in how buyers view you as a seller.

If you just toss your items into a box or envelope, it's going to leave a sour taste in your buyers' minds. Their purchases are likely to arrive damaged or with bumped and scuffed up packaging that looks like it's been run through the wringer.

I know many books recommend recycling used boxes, packing materials, and such to use in your shipping. In my mind—that's the worst mistake you can make.

You only get one chance to make an excellent first impression. Suppose your package arrives all scuffed up or with squiggly lines where you crossed out previous addresses. Customers are going to be concerned about their purchases. If that's the way you package stuff, your buyers are going to think, "God help me," about the stuff you put inside the box.

Set Up Your Shipping Station

Most sellers ship their items from the same desk they sell from. If you're a part-time seller, that's okay. If you eBay for a living, I'd recommend a separate shipping station.

Here's why.

Shipping is a specialized task. You need a lot of space and all of your packaging materials and supplies close by to do it right. I have a separate desk and table set up for shipping. My shipping computer is only used when I'm shipping items or tracking shipments. It's an older castoff, but it serves the purpose. I have two printers hooked up to it...a Zebra LP 2844 and a Samsung laser printer.

Most of my shipping labels get printed on the Zebra. I use the laser printer to print packing slips and thank you cards. I also have a postal scale that attaches to the computer through the USB port. It's digital and can accurately weigh up to twenty-five pounds in one-ounce increments. The weight is automatically transferred into Stamps.com with one click of my mouse, so there's never any guesswork involved. I usually round up to the next ounce to add a little wiggle room for tape or the label.

I have sturdy warehouse shelving set up opposite to my desk. The bottom row has flat boxes in various sizes, and the next shelf has priority mail boxes and envelopes. The shelf above that has stay-flat mailers and padded mailers. The top shelf has all of my miscellaneous supplies—shipping labels, paper, extra rolls of tape, box cutters, and Sharpie markers.

Everything is close by. Once I get started, I can typically package and ship thirty or forty items in an hour, and I'm done. Before I had my shipping station, it always took twice as long because I ran from here to there looking for stuff or finding a good spot to spread my stuff out.

Must-Have Supplies

There are specific supplies you need to keep on hand so you can ship smart.

>> **Packaging material**. Stock up on boxes, padded mailers, stay-flat mailers, bubble wrap, and tape. The worst thing that can happen is to be in the middle of packaging up your orders and then discover you don't have the supplies you need.

If you ship priority or express mail, stop by the post office and pick up the supplies you need. Better yet, hop online and check out https://store.usps.com/store/browse/category.jsp?categoryId=shipping-supplies.

Order your boxes ten, twenty-five, or more at a time, depending upon how quickly you go through them. The post office will deliver them free within two to three days.

If you need to purchase boxes, padded mailers, or stay-flat mailers—consider Uline http://www.uline.com/. They have reasonable prices and quick delivery.

Wal-Mart carries a great selection of boxes in their shipping supply aisle. The prices are reasonable, especially when you compare them to the big box office supply stores.

I've also had good luck buying supplies from several suppliers on eBay.

. Value Mailers
http://stores.ebay.com/VALUEMAILERS?_trksid=p2047675.l2563

. Royal Mailers
http://stores.ebay.com/Royalmailers?_trksid=p2047675.l2563

>> **Postal scale**. If you sell online, you need a postal scale. Many sellers fudge it and just guess at weights. Trust me. No one is that good. Every ounce you guess wrong costs you at least seventeen cents—over a year, that's going to easily be a hundred bucks or more.

Buy a good digital scale. Weight capacities start at five pounds. I recommend choosing a scale from USPS.com. They have a good selection, and the scales hold up well.

>> **Printer**. The printer you use is a matter of preference. I use a Zebra label printer because it prints a small compact label you can peel off and stick on your package. There's no messing with tape or ink cartridges because it's a thermal printer. The next best choice is a laser printer. The ink is less expensive, and it prints quicker. There's nothing more aggravating than waiting for a slow inkjet printer to finish printing your label. The last choice is an inkjet printer. It's

slow, but it will get the job done. If you use adhesive-backed labels, an inkjet printer is your best bet. Whenever I tried them in my laser printer, they were too thick and jammed it up.

>> **Shipping tape**. I used to buy my tape at Sam's Club or Wal-Mart. If you have an eBay store, get it from them. Sellers get a quarterly credit for shipping supplies that you can use for tape or packaging materials. My only recommendation is not to buy the cheapest tape you can find. It tears, it splits, and it's a mess restarting the roll.

>> **Bubble wrap**. If you're packaging china, old books, or other fragile items, you're going to need bubble wrap. Here's one item it's okay to reuse. Good places to purchase bubble wrap are Sam's Club, Wal-Mart, or online.

>> **Box cutter**. Be sure to keep a couple of box cutters and plenty of extra razor blades on hand. You want to package your items right. The best way to do that is to give everything a snug, tight fit. To do that, you need a box cutter with a sharp blade so you can easily refit boxes.

>> **Peanuts** are those little white foam half-circles shippers use to line their packages. They're all static-filled and stick to everything. I hate them and refuse to buy anything from

sellers that use them. Use peanuts at your own risk. They're a sticky mess.

Packaging Tips

Okay. You've set up your shipping station and stocked up on supplies. Now it's time for *Packaging 101*.

The best tip I can give you is to always choose the right type of packaging. Err on the side of more packing materials, not less. This is one area you don't want to skimp on.

Tip #1. Choose the correct type of packaging. If you're shipping a newer book or a paperback, it's okay to use a padded mailer. If you're shipping a rare book or vintage book, you need to package it differently. Use a box, make sure it is placed inside a sealed plastic bag, and then wrap it with newspaper or bubble wrap. This keeps the corners from getting scuffed or bent, and it protects the book from moisture damage should your box get exposed to water.

If you're shipping china, glass figurines, or other fragile materials, pick a box about six inches larger all around than what you are shipping. Line the box with bubble wrap or wadded up newspapers. Next, wrap each item in bubble wrap or newspaper and tape it up, so it is secure. Lay the item in the box and cover it with bubble wrap or newspaper. Continue doing this until the box is full. Build another layer of bubble wrap or wadded up newspapers at the top. You'll know you've got it right when you shake the box. If you feel stuff shifting around, open the box and add more packing material.

When you ship electronics, laptops, or tablets, your best bet is to ship them in the original box. If that isn't possible, find a box slightly larger than the item you're going to ship. Build a nest in the box using foam, bubble wrap, or wadded-up newspapers. Place your item in a sealed plastic bag to prevent moisture damage. Wrap it several times with bubble wrap. Place the item in the box. Wrap any accessories, discs, power cord, etc., separately and place them in the box. Build a nest around the top of the box before you seal it to ensure the item won't get shaken in transit. Tape the box length-wise and width-wise. This ensures that the tape won't break free where the box can come open in shipment.

If you ship clothes, you can pop a shirt or t-shirt into a priority mailbag. If you're shipping jackets, jeans, or multiple items, use a flat rate priority mailbox to reduce your costs. If you're unsure which is cheaper—regular priority mail or flat rate, weigh it out and let the numbers do the talking.

I'm not going to describe any more scenarios. Just understand that you need to adapt every packing situation to the item you are shipping.

I've received close to a thousand packages over the last fifteen years. Some of them were perfectly packed, some were adequate, and quite a few arrived banged up and had the items I purchased hanging halfway out of the box or missing.

Tip #2. The best time to decide how to pack an item for shipment is before you list it.

Think about it. If you list a computer or rare figurine, how will you determine shipping charges if you don't know how you're going to pack and ship it?

I have hundreds of rare newspapers dating from 1806 to the Civil War period. However, I don't have a cost-effective way to ship individual papers to buyers. If I fold the paper to make the size manageable, I ruin a good part of the item's collectability. To ship a single paper would require me to buy an oversized casing for it and then a custom box to put it in. Packaging could quickly run forty to fifty dollars before shipping costs. That's a hefty chunk of change to add to a paper I'm selling for twenty-five dollars.

The economics don't work out in this case, so the papers remain in my private collection for now.

Make sure you don't go underwater on the items you sell. Before you list an item, assess what it's going to take to ship it. What kind of packaging materials do you need? How much is shipping likely to cost? Is the item expensive enough to require insurance? If so, how much is that going to cost?

Know what you're looking at upfront because you can't come back and ask the customer for more money after the sale.

A lot of sellers box their items up at the time they list them. They weigh the package, input the weight into the eBay shipping calculator, and all of the hard work is done. If the item sells, they grab the box, print a label, and drop it in the mail.

Do whatever works for you.

Just keep in mind buyers always have questions. You may need to open the box to answer a question or shoot a quick picture or two. Also, not every item sells. You may need to bundle that item up with several other items to make a sale.

Do I Need to Offer Free Shipping?

Free shipping is the biggest bugaboo-facing online sellers right now.

eBay encourages sellers to offer free shipping, and they promote items with free shipping to buyers. Because of this, many new sellers think they have to offer free shipping. Let me assure you: that's not true.

You don't have to offer free shipping on any of the items you sell. However, you may want to offer free shipping. Here's why?

Typically sales increase when you offer free shipping. There's something about "free" and "shipping" that makes buyers loosen up their purse strings and spend more money. I'm not sure what it is, but the word "free" is one of those magical keys that can get consumers to pull the trigger and spend more money.

Keep that info tucked away in the back of your head for a moment.

Just because eBay likes free shipping and consumers like free shipping doesn't mean it's the magical ingredient you've been searching for to increase your sales and profits. It needs to be the right combination that's good for both of you. You need to make a profit, and your customer needs to get a good value when you offer free shipping.

How does that work?

If you sell lightweight, easy-to-ship items, free shipping should be a no-brainer. Let me repeat that. If you sell light items that you can ship for under a dollar, give your customers free shipping rather than trying to charge them that buck. If you sell postcards, baseball cards, small knickknacks, and inexpensive jewelry items that you can mail in a regular envelope—mark your item up a buck. Give your customer free shipping.

If you sell heavier items, low margin items, or custom-made items, free shipping may make sense. Before you pull the trigger, though, do your research. Investigate what other sellers with similar items are doing. If everyone else is offering free shipping, you're better off following the pack, unless...and, this is a big unless. If other sellers have marked their items up enough to cover shipping, it might make sense to charge shipping and price your item as low as you can while still holding a decent profit.

If sellers in your category are split, with some offering free shipping and some charging for shipping, you may want to test the waters. Offer a few items with free shipping and a few with your regular shipping charges. Run with the method that makes the most sales for you.

If you're the only one selling a particular product and you're making a killer profit, go ahead and give your customers free shipping. It's extra icing on the cake. It's one more reason to buy from you.

Setting Shipping Rates in eBay

Setting shipping rates is another tricky area that can confuse sellers.

Here's the least you need to know.

- eBay requires top-rated sellers to provide tracking information for domestic sales. You are also required to post tracking information back into the listing on a minimum of 90% of the items you sell.
- Top-rated Sellers are required to ship their items with a one-day handling period to receive all the Top-rated seller benefits.
- If you sell an item valued at over $200, you must provide signature delivery confirmation.

If you're not a Top-rated Seller, it's still a good idea to provide delivery confirmation on every item you ship. It protects you from bad buyers who may open an item not received case because they know they will win if you can't provide proof of delivery.

Now we'll get down to the nitty-gritty of setting up shipping in your item listings.

To set your domestic shipping options, look for the section labeled *add shipping details* on your sell your item form.

The first choice you need to make is to select your shipping method from the drop-down box. There are four possible choices: flat cost, calculated freight, and no shipping—local pickup. Flat cost is where you charge all buyers the same shipping rate. Calculated shipping uses the eBay shipping calculator to figure shipping based upon your item weight and where it is being shipped to. Freight is for larger items too big to ship by USPS or UPS. Items shipping by freight are carried by a semi or common carrier.

If you sell large items that need to ship by common carrier, keep in mind that eBay's freight calculator only works up to 150 pounds. If your item exceeds that weight, you need to use flat rate shipping. You also need to understand a few things about truck lines. Most carriers only require their drivers to pull your item to the back of the truck. It's up to your customer to have people available to help them get their item out of the truck and carry it inside the house.

Explain this to your customers in your listing description. Explain it again in the shipping instructions you send the buyer after the sale. Here's another tip. You can request the truck line to call your customer the day before delivery. Sometimes they do it; sometimes, they don't, so try not to make too many promises.

To set up calculated shipping, click the blue lettering that says *calculate shipping*. This will open a pop-up box. Fill in the options, and you're good to go.

If you are using flat rate shipping, click in the box that says standard shipping. Select the shipping service you want to set up, and enter the shipping fee in the smaller box to the right where it says cost. If you want to offer free shipping for that service, put a checkmark where it says free shipping. To offer more shipping options, click the blue lettering that says *offer additional service*.

To offer local pickup, check the box where it says *Local Pickup*. Be careful when you select this option because local pickup is not available in all categories.

Think long and hard before you offer local pick up for your items. Do you really want to invite customers into your house? Over the years, I've had some local buyers insist on picking up their items to save on shipping. Most times, I've delivered the items to their business or met the customer outside McDonald's or another local business. It's less risky but a significant pain in the backside.

Avoid local pickup whenever possible.

If you set up flat shipping rules, you can check the box to apply them. If you would like to set up or edit your rules, click on the blue lettering that says *edit rules*. The pop-up box will walk you through setting up shipping discounts. If you edit the top set of rules, the changes are only good for the listing you are currently working on. If you want to create a discount for all of your listings, you need to scroll down to the bottom of the pop-up box where it says Promotional Shipping Rule (applies to all items).

If you haven't used this feature before, I would suggest giving it a whirl. You'd be surprised at how many buyers will shop for additional items to save a few bucks on shipping.

The next choice you have is to select the *handling time*. If you're a Top-rated seller, you must ship all items within one day so be sure to select that option.

The final item gives you a nudge to add next-day shipping to your listing. I don't offer the service unless buyers contact me and say they absolutely have to have next-day shipping. My reason for not offering next-day shipping is very few people request it, and you have deadlines you need to meet. It takes more effort than it's worth.

That's it. Your shipping options are set.

Here's another quick tip, so you don't have to go through this with every item you list. Set up one of your listings as a template, or when you list new items, pull up one of your old listings and select the option to sell a similar item. When you use either of these options, all your previous info transfers over to the new listings. Use the info you want to keep, type over or delete the unwanted info.

Printing Shipping Labels Using eBay & PayPal

Both eBay and PayPal let sellers print shipping labels directly from their sites. The process is easy to use and allows you to print professional-looking labels and invoices to include with your shipments.

Print eBay Shipping Labels

The easiest way to print shipping labels using eBay is to go into your *Seller Hub*. The first column on the left-hand side says *Tasks*. Click on the number opposite where it says *Print labels and ship*.

That will bring up a list of your sold items. Locate the item you want to ship, and click on them.

When you select *Print Shipping*, it takes you to the eBay ship your item page. When you click into it, the page is prepopulated with all of your item information.

You're shown the item description, the price paid, shipping fee, shipping service paid for, and the expected delivery date at the top of the page. The right-hand column contains the shipping information—the buyer's address and your address. If you need to change either address, select where it says change, and enter the correct shipping information.

Over to the right, towards the bottom of the page, is a section that says *Additional options*. I choose *add a message* and write a standard thank you message here. You can also use it to tell your buyer a little more about the item or direct them to your store specials. It's up to you.

The center column contains the package details. It's where you choose the carrier, add shipping options, and choose your mailing date. eBay has three approved carriers, the United States Postal Service (USPS), UPS, and FedEx. My shipping experience has all been with the USPS, so that's what I'm going to cover here. If you ship using FedEx or UPS, select them as the carrier and follow the prompts to complete your shipment.

The first thing you need to do is select your carrier. In this case, choose USPS.

Use the next box to select your shipping service. The choices are priority mail, first-class package, parcel select, media mail, and priority mail express. The priority mail and priority mail express options let you choose the level of service you want.

After you've selected your service, you have the option of printing the auction number or some other message on the label. If you want to do this, check the box, and type in your message. The default message is the auction id.

The final box lets you choose the mailing date. You can choose today, tomorrow, or the next day. The reason for this is you're supposed to mail your package the same day you print the label, so if you're printing the label today but not mailing your package for two days, you should change the date. I've never had a problem with the post office if I'm a day or two late dropping the package in the mail, but now you know the correct way to do it.

The third column shows your postage cost broken down by the postage cost, the delivery confirmation fee, and the total cost. Below, you can hide the shipping so buyers can't see how much actual shipping cost you. It's your choice—if you're playing by the rules and charging actual shipping, let your buyers see the shipping cost. It will prove you're on the up-and-up.

When you're done, click purchase postage. When you do this, your PayPal account will be charged for the shipping fees. The next screen will show a mockup of the label. You can print a sample or print the label.

The program automatically transfers tracking information into the item listing so buyers can follow their package's movement as it is being shipped to them.

Alternatively, you can print your postage labels directly from PayPal. Open your PayPal account and locate the transaction you want to print the postage for to get started. Click on the text where it says *Print shipping label*. It brings up the same shipping page we used above, so you can follow through using those directions. (Note: This item no longer works if you use eBay's managed payments.)

Do I Need Insurance?

When eBay allowed sellers to charge customers for insurance, I required all my buyers to purchase it. It saved a lot of hassles. If the item was lost, the customer was taken care of.

After shipping over 30,000 items, I discovered that very few items are lost, stolen, or damaged in transit. I think I've had two damaged packages and three lost packages in fifteen years. So is insurance really necessary? It depends on you and your tolerance for loss. Most of the items I ship cost between twenty to twenty-five dollars—insurance costs close to two bucks for each package. Take two bucks times thirty thousand packages, and that's close to sixty thousand dollars.

My losses in all this time have amounted to under one hundred bucks. If I'd bought insurance on every item, I shipped I'd be out close to 60,000 dollars. When you look at it that way—insuring my packages doesn't make sense.

But…insuring my more expensive packages does make me feel all warm and fuzzy inside. Because of that, I decided to pick a number where I would insure my shipments. If the value exceeds that number, I purchase insurance. For me, the magic number is one-hundred dollars. For you, it may be ten dollars or one thousand dollars. Choose your threshold for loss, then insure all shipments that exceed that number. That way, you can sleep at night.

Here's the least you need to know about insurance.

- eBay doesn't allow sellers to charge buyers for insurance. You can roll it into your shipping costs, or you can bury it in the cost of your item.
- Filing an insurance claim with the Post Office is a pain in the rear end. It takes a minimum of thirty days for the post office to reimburse you. Many times it can take two or three times that long.
- When you sell something on eBay, it's hard to prove an item's actual value, especially for collectibles and one-of-a-kind items. Just because you paid five bazillion dollars for a rare candy bar wrapper doesn't mean that's the value of your item.
- You may have insurance, but your customer doesn't care about that. They don't want to wait thirty days or more to get their money back. If you make them wait for a refund, odds are you're going to receive negative feedback.

With all of that said, how do you file an insurance claim? The easiest way is to do it online. Go to the following link https://www.usps.com/ship/file-domestic-claims.htm. It will walk you through filing an insurance claim for a lost parcel.

Here are a few of the highlights to keep in mind.

You need to upload tracking info for the item, a copy of the sales receipt or your eBay auction listing number (to prove value), and your insurance receipt. If you received a damaged item, you need to save the item and all packaging materials until the claim is completed.

If for some reason, you can't file the claim online, call (800) 275-8777, and they will send you a claim form.

Using a Third-Party Shipping Provider

eBay's shipping label service is great, but sometimes you need a little more oomph to boost your sales and simplify things even more.

I've used Stamps.com for nearly ten years, and it's been an excellent alternative for me. Other people have had good luck using Endicia to handle their shipping needs. Both services charge a monthly service fee for using them.

I know what you're thinking. Wait a minute, Nick, I'm trying to save money, not spend even more.

Believe me, I understand. The thing is, I actually save a lot of money using Stamps.com to power my eBay shipping. Here's why I use it and how it saves me money.

What got me hooked on Stamps.com is it's the only way I can ship my items first class international without going to the post office and having them print labels for me. If you use eBay's shipping solution or Click-N-Ship®, you can only ship internationally using priority or express mail. When I do that, international sales go down because of the extra shipping costs involved. The extra sales I get by offering the less expensive shipping solution offsets the $15.99 monthly fee.

I like using Stamps.com because it collects information from all of the platforms I sell on. Then, it lets me handle shipping from one central location. That means I can ship the items I sell on eBay and Amazon from the same program console.

I don't have to jump from site to site to ship everything. If I need to look up shipping info for an item—it's all in Stamps.com.

It's convenient. I like that. It's worth the extra fifteen dollars a month it costs me to use the service.

To get started with Stamps.com, click on the following link http://www.stamps.com/. Select get started to register for a new account. They often offer a sign-up special that gives you a free postal scale, $25.00 in free shipping credits, and miscellaneous other goodies, along with a one-month free trial.

Once you're good to go, you can connect all of your seller accounts.

Next, I will give you a quick walk-through on how to connect your seller accounts and how to print postage using Stamps.com. (I assume Endicia works the same way, but I've never used that service, so I can't provide you with specifics.)

Don't worry. I'll make this quick and painless.

Setup Shipping Accounts

There are two ways to set up your accounts. Select *Manage Sources* in the toolbar at the top of the screen, or select *batch* from the toolbar in the left-hand column.

Choose Create Profile, and select the data source you want to create.

Printing Postage

When you open your Stamp.com dashboard, there is a command bar running across the top of the screen. There are four main tabs that you'll use over and over again: import orders, manage sources, print, and add order.

- Import orders lets you collect your orders from all of the sites you sell on and bring them into Stamps.com.
- Manages sources lets you add, delete, or edit data streams.
- Add order allows you to print a label for a package where the customer is not included in any of your data streams. An example is when I send out a review copy of one of my books. The recipient is not in my data stream, so I need to set up a one-time shipment.

- Print pulls up the screen to print your shipping label.

Okay, let's assume you just sat down at your desk, and you're ready to start shipping. What do you do?

Select <import orders> from the top menu bar; you'll be prompted several times about actions that are in progress. Most often, Stamps.com wants permission to update addresses to match the official address in the postal system computer. Click okay.

After a while, your orders will appear in a spreadsheet in the middle of the screen. Select the item you want to mail, and click on the recipient name. This will open up the shipping screen for that customer.

Off to the left-hand side of the screen, you will see your name and address. Below that, you will find your customer's name and address. You can make whatever changes you need to the shipping address here. The next line is labeled email address. Check the box in front of it, and it will populate with your customer's email address. When you check this, it will send shipping and tracking info to your buyer. The box right after this is the cost code. You can make an internal note here if you are tracking categories for shipping.

The next column contains your shipping options.

If you have a USB scale, it will transfer the weight with the click of a button. I usually round up to the next ounce or two, depending on the item I'm shipping. That gives me a little wiggle room for the label and tape.

After this, you need to choose the type of mailpiece—package, thick envelope, etc.

Then you select the mail class –

- First Class
- Priority Mail
- Express Mail
- Parcel Post
- Media Mail

Place a checkmark in the tab to select the mail class. When you do this, it will show the cost of that service. Some classes are blanked out if you can't choose them to ship that particular item. Packages over thirteen ounces cannot be shipped by first class, so that shipping method would not be available for you to select.

After this, choose tracking options. Delivery confirmation is free with most shipping methods, signature confirmation (for an additional charge), or none (tracking is not available on flats sent by first class).

Just below this, there is a line labeled options. This is where you can add—certified, USPS insurance, registered, or COD delivery.

The next option lets you select insurance. You can select none or Stamps.com. Your final choice is whether you want to hide the postage cost so buyers cannot see it. If you marked your shipping up a lot, be sure to choose this option.

After selecting your options, click <save> at the bottom of the box. A green circle should appear in front of the <order id> on the spreadsheet. Choose <print> from the menu bar at the top of the screen. You should see a pop-up that shows the printer's name and details. Select <print> at the bottom of the screen to print your label.

International Shipping with Stamps.com

Setting up an order for international delivery is very similar to shipping a domestic order. The only difference is you need to complete a customs form.

Here's how to fill out the online customs form.

Click on the customs form. It will display a pop-up box for you to fill out. At the top of the form, it asks for a phone number. If your customer listed a number, it will prepopulate. If they did not give a phone number, type 999-999-9999, otherwise it will not let you continue.

Where it asks for contents, you are given several options. Choose <merchandise>. In the box next to this type a short description. I usually type article or print.

About midway down the page, there is a section labeled *itemized package contents*. The first box asks for the quantity or number of items in your package. After that, you're asked for a short description of the item. It should prepopulate from your eBay item description. If the description is too long, you need to shorten it, or the form will not process correctly. The next item it asks you for is the weight of just the item (without the packaging).

When you've completed all of the items, the box at the end of this line asks *add item*. Check that box, and it will move your description into the box below that line.

At the bottom of the pop-up box is a form you need to check. It begins with "I acknowledge..." Once you select the check box, the pop-up box disappears, and you can print your item like normal.

Sell International

Here's a secret many online sellers don't know. The fastest-growing sellers on eBay are powering that growth with international sales. According to a recent article on Linnworks, "76% of [the] fastest growers are primarily trading across borders."

The beauty of selling internationally is when the domestic economy slows down, there are still pockets of growth and increasing demand in foreign economies. The key to tapping into these growth pockets is to make your items available to sellers in those countries.

I started listing items internationally in 2001. Within a year, thirty to thirty-five percent of my orders were shipping overseas. I completed nearly 5,000 international transactions over the past twenty years with only two lost packages.

If you're on the line about getting started with international shipping—consider baby-stepping it. Start with proven foreign trade partners like Canada, the United Kingdom, and Australia. There are few language barriers dealing with these countries. You should also consider selling to Germany. According to a recent article in *Forbes Magazine*, Germany and the United Kingdom account for 48 percent of all international sales made on eBay.

To qualify for international visibility, sellers must meet several standards.

- Have a verified PayPal account tied to their eBay seller account. If you are on managed payments, things requirements are somewhat different.
- PayPal must be offered as a payment option
- Must have 10 or more positive feedbacks
- Items must be listed in the appropriate category
- Need to enable shipping to countries you want to ship in
- For best visibility, sellers must specify the levels of shipping service they are offering

If you sell using your eBay.com account, your feedback will be visible to sellers on eBay's foreign sites.

Suppose you are a seller in the United States and specify you will ship to Canada. In that case, your items will automatically be listed on eBay.ca.

Items listed on international sites do not count as duplicate listings, so sellers are not penalized for listing the same item on different eBay sites.

eBay gives you four ways to make your items available to international buyers.

1. Opt into eBay's Global Shipping Program.
2. Enable your items for international shipping.
3. List your items on international sites.
4. Open eBay stores in countries where you do a large amount of business.

What I'm going to do next is look at each option in more detail and explain who it is for and how you can get started using it.

eBay Global Shipping Program

FYI: There's one thing you've got to think about before you go it alone and ship international packages yourself. COVID-19.

Some countries no longer allow packages from certain countries to enter their borders. Several months ago, I received an eBay message that one of my international sales was canceled. The country it was shipping to rejected it.

eBay refunded the buyer's payment and let me know the package would not be returned. That was sort of a bummer. Then, they added that I wouldn't be charged for the return.

If you ship internationally using eBay's Global Shipping Program, you're protected. If you ship packages internationally on your own, you're shit-out-of-luck. You lose your money and merchandise.

It's going to take additional research on your part to see which countries allow packages from your country and which ones don't. What makes it more challenging is the list is constantly changing.

You may only want to ship inexpensive items internationally on your own until things sort themselves out.

eBay introduced its Global Shipping Program several years ago. It's an easy way for sellers to jump into international selling without worrying about shipping rules, customs forms, etc.

If you've been itching to get started with international sales but were afraid of the extra work involved, give eBay's Global Shipping Program a try.

Many small sellers are terrified of international shipping. They've heard so many horror stories they're scared to give it a shot. They don't want to fill out customs forms or worry about whether their package is going to make it all the way to Timbuktu or not.

eBay has eliminated all of that grief for sellers who use their Global Shipping Program. Sellers list their items just like they usually would. When the item sells, they ship it to an eBay shipping center in the United States.

Bing Badda boom! As soon as it arrives at the shipping center, your responsibility for the shipment is over. From that point on, eBay and its shipping partners (Pitney Bowes) assume all responsibility for getting your package to its destination.

Here's how it works.

When you list your item for sale on eBay, check the box to include your item in the Global Shipping Program, and you're good to go.

Some categories don't qualify for inclusion in the Global Shipping Program. When you bump into these, eBay will flag the item and let you know. I do a lot of selling in the collectibles category. Collectibles manufactured before 1899 don't qualify, so I see this issue pop up quite often. The only way around it is to ship the item internationally yourself. I'll discuss this option in more detail later.

When an item sells using the Global Shipping Program, sellers can't send the buyer an invoice. eBay takes care of all this for you. The reason is you have no way of knowing what their shipping fee will be.

Once the customer pays, you receive your payment notice along with the address to ship your item to. An easy way to recognize a payment made through the Global Shipping Program is the address will include a long reference number.

Ship your item like you usually would. Include delivery confirmation so you can be sure the item was received at the shipping center. Once you receive delivery confirmation, your part in the transaction is complete.

eBay's shipping partner—Pitney Bowes—will readdress the item, fill out all of the appropriate customs forms, and ensure your item is delivered to the customer.

That's the way it should happen. Every now and then, things don't work out as planned—the customer doesn't receive the item, or it arrives damaged. As a seller, you're supposed to be protected from receiving negative feedback in such a situation. That's true to a point. You need to keep an eye on your feedback profile and keep after eBay to update it when errors are made.

I received negative feedback due to a customer not receiving their item. I knew it wasn't received because that's what the seller wrote in his feedback. So I called eBay customer service and explained the problem. After about fifteen minutes of researching the problem, the rep agreed I was not responsible. He removed the negative feedback while we were still on the phone.

If you experience a similar problem, contact eBay customer service immediately. When you call, have the listing item number and the feedback information available and ready to share with them. Make it easy for eBay to help you.

Overall the Global Shipping Program is a great way to increase your sales. At my peak selling period, international sales accounted for roughly thirty-five to forty percent of my eBay sales and profits.

If you're looking for an effortless method to grow your sales, opt into the Global Shipping Program and give it a shot.

Enable Items for International Shipping

We've already talked about eBay's Global Shipping Program and how easy it is to use, so why would anybody want to ship international packages on their own?

That's a great question.

It comes down to having more control over your shipping options and making more sales. eBay's Global Shipping Program figures in custom fees, a markup to pay themselves and their shipping partner an additional profit, plus actual shipping costs. The final number eBay shows your customer for shipping can be mind-boggling and cost you the sale.

Let me use the products I sell as an example. When I ship items internationally, I charge $5.00 to ship items to Canada and $9.00 for shipping anywhere else in the world. Sometimes I make a few extra bucks, sometimes I lose a few bucks, but over time it averages out. Keep in mind, the buyer is still on the line for duty and customs fees when their item arrives.

When I sell the same item using eBay's Global Shipping Program, they charge Canadian customers in the low twenty dollar range. Customers in Europe and the rest of the world pay thirty dollars or more. My items typically sell for sixteen to twenty-five dollars, so customers face some serious sticker shock when they're hit with eBay's shipping price.

Self-preservation is the primary reason I ship most international packages myself.

Now, I'm going to walk you through setting up the international portion of your eBay sell your item form. It's structured very similarly to how you set up your domestic shipping options, so it should be easy to follow along and use.

Everything you need to set your international shipping options can be found in the box labeled *International Shipping*.

The first choice you are offered is to opt into the Global Shipping Program. Check this box.

Below this, you have a drop-down box that offers *additional shipping options*. It gives you the option to select flat rate, calculated shipping, or no additional options. As a quick review, flat rate shipping is where you have one fixed shipping fee for all buyers. Calculated shipping uses the eBay shipping calculator to determine the shipping price based on where you are shipping your item. The difference is—flat rate shipping is easier to set up and use. Calculated shipping gives buyers closer to you a break in shipping costs, thus allowing you to grab additional sales from price-conscious buyers.

After you choose your shipping method, you'll see another drop-down box that says shipping. It gives you three choices: worldwide, chose custom location, or Canada. I usually set up a separate price for worldwide and Canada—any more is overkill in my book. However, if you ship many packages to Mexico, the UK, or wherever, go ahead and set up a special price for them too. The drop-down box next to this lets you choose the type of service you wish to offer, and the box to the right of that lets you set your shipping price.

In the *additional ship to locations*, you can check off areas you are willing to ship to, and the buyer can contact you for more details. Some sellers have lots of rules about where they will and will not ship too. Many sellers mark Malaysia, Italy, Mexico, Russia, etc., off-limits based on other people's problems. I've shipped items to all of those countries and never had a problem. Before you mark these areas off-limits or discourage buyers from specific regions, wait until you have a problem, then evaluate the situation and determine how you want to handle it.

The final line—combined shipping discounts, lets you apply your discount rules to this purchase if you set them up. My items are light and generally only add a few ounces to the package; therefore, I ship all additional items for free. It's a great way to encourage buyers to continue shopping with you. If you can't offer to ship all additional items for free—consider offering some type of discounted shipping for additional purchases. It will bring you more business over the long haul.

That's it. You're open for international business. Sit back and wait for the orders to roll in.

I'm going to make one additional suggestion here. Take a few moments to help set buyer expectations. International buyers are similar to domestic buyers—they want to purchase their items today and receive them yesterday.

Most times, shipping goes smoothly, and items arrive on time. Still, there are many circumstances beyond your control, especially when dealing with international customers.

I usually post the following information in each of my listings and include it again in my shipping emails.

"Normal international delivery time is eight to fifteen business days. It can take as long as four to six weeks—depending upon customs and other shipping issues. Please be patient, and take this into consideration when placing your orders."

It helps to set buyer expectations before the order is placed. If customers ask where their item is, you can refer them back to the info posted in your listing. By giving realistic delivery time frames, you're going to save yourself a lot of grief and wasted emails trying to explain why customers haven't received their packages yet.

Remember—International customers really have you over the barrel. Tracking is virtually nonexistent for international shipments. The post office is experimenting with international delivery confirmation to select countries, but the service is spotty at best. There's no guarantee the mailman in Canada or the UK will actually scan your package when he drops it off. He may be having a bad day, or he may be trying to outrun a dog. If your customer files an item not received case, you're going to lose because there's no way to provide proof of delivery.

Sorry to be the one to break it to you, but it's a fact of life when you're doing business on eBay. I've only had this happen once. A buyer in Germany opened an item not received case two days after paying for his item. There was no possible way it could travel from Iowa to Germany in two days.

Guess what? It didn't matter. eBay and PayPal decided the case against me because I didn't have proof of delivery. As I said, this happened one time out of five thousand international shipments, so it's not a big deal.

One other quick comment here—many sellers assume proof of shipping is enough to win an international case. It's not. A stamped customs form from your post office is of no help to you if the buyer files an item not received case. If you can't show proof your item was delivered, you don't have a leg to stand on.

Using eBay's Global Shipping option is a win-win for buyers and sellers. eBay alerts you when your item reaches their fulfillment center and again when it is delivered.

List Your Items on International Sites

What we've talked about so far involves listing your items on eBay.com and making them available to buyers in foreign countries. This works because eBay.com is the largest of the eBay sites and has the most listings posted to it. As a result, many international buyers search here first when they're looking for new items.

If you do a lot of business with certain countries, you may increase sales by listing items directly on that site.

If you're a registered eBay user, you can sell on any of eBay's international sites. To get started, just log in with your current ID and password, and start listing your items. Sellers with anchor stores can list on international sites for free. Sellers without an anchor store are charged listing fees if they exceed their free limits

If you want to make more sales, there are a few details you should consider.

1. What language are you going to use?

If you sell in Canada, the United Kingdom, or Australia—English might be fine. But, the UK and Australia use different dialects, and the meanings for words are not always the same. Canada has a sizeable French-speaking population, so you need to consider them, too. Should you post in English and French?

If you post your listing in Germany, France, or Japan—what do you do? Many buyers there speak English as a second language, but do you want to leave their understanding to chance?

It's a tough call. You can use Google Translate or Bing Translate to write your description. The translations are usually stilted and hard to read. A better choice would be to find a native language translator on Fiverr or odesk. They would be able to provide you with a more accurate translation.

If you sell low dollar value or one-of-a-kind items, the translation apps are going to be your most cost-effective option. If you sell more expensive items, a translator can help you create more professional-sounding listings that will make more sales. Look at it as an investment in your success.

Other sellers rely on translation apps. eBay offers several of these apps that you can place in your item description. One app is called *One Hour Translation*, and the other is *Translation for Worldwide*. You can read more about them in the app guide at the end of this chapter.

2. What about the title?

Are the keywords and the context the same in German, Spanish, and other languages as they are in the United States?

Do you know what terms someone in Germany would use to search for an iPad or a smartphone? When they're looking for a denim jacket, what other terms would they search on?

Your title is how potential buyers discover your item. If you don't know the local dialect or slang, how do you know the best words to use in your title?

Go back to item one. A translator fluent in the native language would write the most appropriate title for your item listings.

3. What are you going to charge for shipping?

Do you charge international rates, offer free shipping, or split it somewhere in the middle?

Shipping is a critical ingredient in determining how successful you'll be at international selling. The good news is items just about always make it to their destination. The bad news is sometimes packages take forever to arrive at their destination.

When I listed items on eBay.uk several years ago, I marked my items up a bit and offered free shipping. A funny thing happened—most of my items ended up selling to my regular customers here in the United States. It wasn't quite what I expected, but sales did go up.

After a month, I switched tactics and offered a low-cost international shipping option—five dollars, compared to the nine dollar rate I charged on eBay.com. Once I did that, I started getting more buyers from the U. K.

Joseph Dattilo, the founder of Virtualbotix, LLC, explained their shipping options. "We offer USPS and UPS shipping providers and generally have First Class International, Priority International, Priority Express International, and UPS International as an option. Initially, we only had First Class International as an option. However, we found that very few high-value items were sold. We were contacted by dozens of buyers who demanded that we make other methods available.

"Since offering USPS Priority Mail International and Priority Mail Express International, we have seen a dramatic increase in sales of items whose value is greater than $100. The interesting thing is that the boost to sales occurred, but the use of these more expensive services is still rather rare. Customers seem more likely to buy knowing they have the option to get it fast, but often still choose the most economical shipping method."

The final takeaway is sellers can benefit from offering a wider variety of shipping options, even if their customers decide not to take advantage of them.

4. How are you going to approach delivery time?

Even if you explain that your item ships from the United States, many buyers aren't going to understand. All they're going to see is that your item is listed on their home site— eBay.uk or eBay.de.

Shipping time is a tough call with any international shipping method. A lot of my first-class shipments make it to Europe faster than they do across the state. Others seem like they get buried on the proverbial slow boat to China.

The problem is, as a seller, you have no way of knowing which packages are going to get tied up in customs. The best you can do is help to set reliable delivery expectations for your customers.

Offer your customers a variety of mailing options. Then give them time frames for delivery using each service. Tell customers the longest it should take for items to deliver. Their package will often arrive sooner, and customers will be delighted because it was delivered sooner than expected.

5. What currency are you going to post items in?

If you sell on eBay.uk or eBay.de and you price your item in dollars, it will confuse buyers. If you price your item in Pounds Sterling or Euros, you need to keep a close eye on currency fluctuations to make sure you don't end up taking a bath if the market turns. When you go to pull your money out of PayPal, it's a two-step process. You have to convert your currency to US dollars first, and then you can transfer funds to your bank.

6. What about VAT taxes, customs fees, and duties?

Many customers aren't going to understand why they have to pay extra fees and taxes. When you list items on their home site, they don't associate the purchase, triggering additional customs and duty fees.

To prevent negative feedback and multiple returns, explain that your item ships from the United States. Customers are responsible for all customs and duty fees as well as VAT taxes. You need to include the same information in every shipping email.

Joseph Dattilo of Virtuabotix says they adhere to eBay's policy on every international listing and include the following disclaimer in every item description –

"For international orders, please allow for additional time for your products to arrive, or choose one of our expedited services to ensure your product arrives promptly. Basic international shipping can take as much as 30 to 60 days, depending on your country. In contrast, expedited international shipments have guaranteed delivery windows.

"Import duties, taxes, and charges are not included in the item price or shipping cost. These charges are the buyer's responsibility.

"Please check with your country's customs office to determine what these additional costs will be before bidding or buying."

All sellers should include similar wording in their international listings. If you don't include similar wording, eBay may decide a buyer protection case against you, citing extended delivery times or additional fees for customs.

Open an International eBay Store

Suppose you're serious about international selling and have a target market in mind. In that case, it might make sense to open an international eBay store.

Let's say you're doing a booming business selling vintage concert t-shirts. Your two best international markets are Germany and the United Kingdom. You've just picked up a new line of custom printed t-shirts, hoodies, bikinis, and other apparel items. The new items sell well to buyers who like the vintage look but can't lay down several hundred dollars for a vintage t-shirt.

You know from experience that most customers who buy your vintage look apparel discover it in your eBay store. Sales in the U. K. and Germany aren't taking off. Then, your marketing intern has a light bulb moment. What if you open local eBay stores in those markets so you can cross-promote the vintage look apparel?

Bingo!

The best way to grow an international market is the same way you do it at home. Build an eBay store, and cross-promote your items.

Set up a scrolling gallery at the bottom of every listing that features the vintage look apparel. Mention the vintage look apparel in every listing, and invite customers to explore your eBay store for more great deals.

Set up listing headers that feature the new items. Build a storefront with clickable links to the new categories. Make it bold and visual.

Use markdown Manager to your advantage. Offer free shipping occasionally. Discount different categories every week or every month. Set up promotion boxes to highlight your specials.

If you set up an eBay store in a non-English speaking country, find a translator to set up your listings and titles.

An eBay store is a slightly more expensive way to sell internationally. Still, the payoff could be immense if you can make a go of it.

The key to success is to localize the store to each market you sell in. Cross-promote items as much as possible, and run frequent specials to build your brand.

Customs Forms

Online shipping tools are the easiest way to handle customs forms. When you use the online tools available through eBay, Click-N-Ship, Endicia, or Stamps.com, they walk you through the forms and ensure they are filled out correctly.

If you insist on doing it old-style, here's a quick tutorial on customs forms.

The post office uses two customs forms—form 2976 and form 2976-A. Form 2976 is required on all international packages weighing less than four pounds, and Form 2976-A is required for all international packages weighing more than four pounds.

Form 2976

Form 2976

The key information needed for each form is –

- Sender's address
- Recipient address
- Value of each item enclosed
- Total value of all items enclosed
- Description of contents
- Senders signature

You are given several choices to describe the contents, including gift, document, commercial sample, other. You need to check other and then describe the contents in the description box.

Often sellers will ask you to lie about the value or check the gift box, so they don't have to pay duty fees (taxes). If you are caught doing this, it is a felony—subject to fines and jail time. If you're tempted to fudge the form for them, ask yourself—is the extra sale worth the penalties you could face?

That's pretty much all there is to it.

Have the post office walk you through your first customs form. After doing it once or twice, you'll be a pro and wonder why you ever worried about international shipping.

Form 2976 A

Form 2976A

Remember, form 2976 A is for international packages that weigh over four pounds or contain contents valued at over $400.

Here's the information needed to fill out form 2976 A.

- Sender's address
- Recipient address
- Value of each item enclosed
- Total value of all items enclosed
- Description of contents
- Senders signature

You are given several choices to describe the contents, including gift, document, commercial sample, other. You need to check other and then describe the contents in the description box.

Getting Down to Business

If you want to be successful selling on eBay, you need to run your eBay store like a business. It will force you to concentrate on the essentials.

Too often, sellers run their business from their personal checking account. They live day-to-day, drawing money from their PayPal account to buy gas or take the family out to dinner.

I've done it. Everybody has.

If you want to be successful, you've got to stop living hand-to-mouth on your eBay earnings.

Use this section as a business primer, then find an accountant or tax professional and have them help you establish your business on the proper footing.

You will make and keep more of the money you take in.

I promise.

What You Need to Know About Taxes

Remember that old saying, "The only thing certain in life is death and taxes." Running a business is all about collecting and paying taxes.

Here are just a few of the different taxes you're going to be dealing with in your eBay business.

1) Sales & use taxes
2) Estimated taxes
3) Self-employment taxes
4) Unemployment tax
5) State and Federal Income Taxes

We're going to talk about each of these taxes. What they are? How they affect your business? And what you need to do to stay on the right side of the IRS and your local tax authorities.

1) **Sales & use taxes**. Forty-five states require residents to pay a sales tax when they purchase merchandise within that state. If you are an online seller and make a sale within your home state, you are required by law to collect the proper sales tax on it and remit the payment to your state tax

authority. Failure to collect sales tax could put you on the wrong side of tax authorities if your sales are audited.

To collect taxes, you need to apply for a sales and use tax permit (sometimes called a resale permit) from your state. There usually is no charge for it, but some states may require you to make a deposit based upon the volume of transactions you are expected to handle.

You will be asked a few quick questions about your business, your sales channel, and your expected sales revenue. Once you receive your permit, you must collect tax on every transaction you process in your home state. Most states base your payment period upon your expected tax collections. As a result, you may have to remit payments monthly, quarterly, or annually.

Use tax is one of the most overlooked or misunderstood taxes. The way it's supposed to work is if you purchase something from outside of your home state and don't pay sales tax, you're supposed to fess up on your state income tax form and pay the appropriate tax. As you can probably guess, that rarely happens.

A good example of an item that would qualify for use tax is if you purchase your mailers from an out-of-state supplier on eBay. They ship them to you without charging sales tax. Because no sales tax was charged on this transaction when you purchased it, you are obligated to pay a use tax to make up for it.

The same thing is true for non-business owners. Suppose you order clothes from a seller on eBay or Amazon and aren't charged sales tax. In that case, you are obligated to declare the transaction on your state income tax return and pay the appropriate sales tax on it.

If you intend to purchase items from a wholesaler, they will require you to provide them with a state tax id. Suppose you can't produce a tax id. In that case, some wholesalers will refuse to do business with you, others will insist on charging you sales tax on all of your purchases. You can also use your tax permit to eliminate sales taxes when purchasing items for resale from other retailers. So the next time you scoop up a cartload of closeouts at the outlet mall, you can save yourself a bundle by not having to pay the sales tax.

Note: Sales tax requirements are currently in a state of flux. Many states now require sellers to collect sales tax whether they have a base of operations there or not. Because of this, eBay has stepped in. They collect sales tax in many states where required and remit the payment directly to the government. That's good and bad for sellers. It's good because there's less hassle and paperwork for sellers to deal with. It's bad because eBay charges sellers fees on the sale tax they collect. If you're a high-volume seller, the extra fees can adversely affect your bottom-line.

2) **Estimated taxes**. If you are self-employed, you must pay estimated taxes to the IRS and your state tax authority. Quarterly taxes are due April 15, July 15, October 15, and January 15. Tax programs such as TurboTax and H R Block will help you estimate your quarterly taxes. If you use GoDaddy Bookkeeping, it will show you your estimated taxes due. GoDaddy also shows your sales tax liability.

Keep in mind most of these programs estimate your taxes based on last year's income. In the case of GoDaddy Bookkeeping, they base their estimates on your trending income. Suppose your income is sporadic or changes from year to year. In that case, you may want to consult with an accountant or tax advisor to ensure you're paying the proper amount.

If you pay in less than a certain percentage of the amount due, you may wind up having to pay extra fees and penalties.

3) **Self-employment taxes** are similar to Social Security and Medicare taxes charged to people who work for an employer. The difference is self-employed persons need to self-report these taxes and pay both the employer's and the employee's share.

Self-employment taxes are figured on Schedule SE of your IRS Form 1040. In 2021 the self-employment tax rate was 15.3% - 12.4% for Social Security and 2.9% for

Medicare. In 2021 the amount of income subject to the Social Security tax portion was capped at $142,800. There is no cap for the Medicare tax portion of self-employment tax.

You can deduct the employer portion of your self-employment tax (approximately 50 percent) when you figure your adjusted gross income for federal taxes.

4) **Unemployment taxes**. If you hire employees, you are required to pay unemployment taxes. These vary by state. Just keep in mind, there is a separate state and Federal tax due.

See Publication 926 for more information and a list of state taxing authorities.
http://www.irs.gov/publications/p926/index.html

5) **Federal and state taxes**. When most online sellers think about taxes, these are what come to mind.

Some online sellers try to avoid paying income taxes on their earnings or think taxes are just for big-time sellers. The truth is if you make as little as one dollar selling online, you are required to report it for income tax purposes.

To keep everyone honest, the government imposed mandatory reporting requirements upon PayPal. If more than $20,000 is deposited into your PayPal account, PayPal is required to report it to the IRS on Form 1099-K.

To view your form 1099-K, sign in to your PayPal Account, hover your pointer over the **history** tab, and this will bring up a drop-down menu. You want to click on **tax documents**, and this will give you the option to view a PDF file of your 1099-K if one was generated for you.

At this time, you are not required to submit the PayPal 1099-K with your income tax filing, but you should be sure you are reporting at least as much income as is shown on it. You can be sure the IRS matches them up and takes a close look at your 1099-K and the income you report on your tax return.

That's the very least you need to know about taxes, and you're online business. Here are a few more tips that can help you out when the time comes to prepare your Federal and state tax forms.

Business income is reported on Schedule C of your Form 1040.

Several tax programs are available to make filing your business taxes easier. The two I've had the most experience working with are TurboTax Business and H R Block Premium or H R Block Premium & Business. Each program conducts a fact-finding interview with you about your business and walks you step-by-step by filing your tax return.

Even if you use an accountant or tax preparer, doing your taxes first can save you hundreds of dollars when it comes time to file your taxes. This way, all of the information is gathered together and entered in the correct areas on your tax return. Your tax professional needs to review everything to make sure nothing is overlooked or left out.

Most Common Tax Deductions

One of the perks of being a business owner is the ability to shift some of your income by taking advantage of various business deductions. Here are some of the most common business deductions taken by online business owners.

Home Office Deduction. Many business owners are afraid to claim the home office deduction because they've heard the IRS targets filers who take it. That is one of those urban legends that get bigger every time it's told.

The home office deduction is every online seller's best friend. It can save you thousands of dollars on your taxes if you use it properly. For the past ten years, I've been able to shield $2140 in income using the home office deduction.

Here are the IRS rules for taking the home office deduction:

1) Your home must be your principal place of business.
2) You must use the area of your home (a room or portion of a room) exclusively to conduct business. If you do all of your work at your kitchen table, you will not qualify for the home office deduction because you don't use that area exclusively for business. Suppose you devote an extra bedroom, basement, or garage exclusively to your online

business activities. In that case, this space will qualify for the home office deduction.

To learn more about the home office deduction, you can check out Publication 587.
http://www.irs.gov/publications/p587/index.html

Mileage Deduction. If you use your vehicle while conducting your business, you can deduct your expenses. Business owners can take either the standard mileage deduction or deduct the actual expenses incurred for using the vehicle in their business.

To take the mileage deduction, you need to record all the miles your car is driven for personal and business use. I would recommend purchasing a mileage log. You can find one in the office supply section at Walmart or Target or at larger office supply stores such as Office Max, Staples, or Office Depot. They run about $3.00 and are small enough to slip under your visor or into your glove box.

Record your beginning and ending mileage whenever you use your car for business. So, next time you go to the post office or stop at a yard sale or estate sale, write your mileage down. It will save you money come April 15.

In 2021 the standard mileage deduction was 56¢ per business mile driven, down from 57.5¢ in 2020. If you opt to deduct actual expenses, record all of your expenses for car payments, insurance, repairs, tires, oil changes, and gasoline. You can then deduct the percentage of expenses based on the miles driven for business usage.

Travel. Did you ever want to visit California or Hawaii but weren't sure you could afford it? Travel costs are fully deductible as long as they are business-related.

Let's say you're ready for a vacation, and eBay is having one of its events in Scottsdale. You can deduct all of your expenses – airfare, car rentals, cabs, motels, food, and admission – as long as they are related to the event. If your spouse helps out in your business, their expenses would be covered as well. Should you decide to make a real vacation of it and bring the kids along, you can't deduct expenses for their travel, food, lodging, etc. You would need to separate their expenses from the rest of your spending.

The travel expense deduction can also be used to cover day trips out of town. If you visit an estate sale or auction several hundred miles away, all your expenses related to the buying trip would be deductible. Again, if you bring along the kids or someone unrelated to your business, their expenses would not be covered.

Computers, printers, office supplies. Are you a techie? Have you always wanted to own the latest, greatest gadgets but wished you had a rich uncle to help you out with the payments?

Uncle Sam can come to the rescue here, too. You can deduct the price of a new computer, printer, cell phone, iPad, or any other gadget you regularly use in your online business. The only hitch is the item needs to be for your business use only.

You have the option of depreciating the expense over the expected life of the item. Or in many cases, you can deduct the total value of the item the year it is purchased.

Internet, cell phone, etc. Suppose you purchase a different cell phone or internet service for your business. In that case, you can deduct the total cost of them as a business expense. If you use them for business and personal use, you can only deduct the portion of the service you use for business.

If you're on track to make a little too much money this year and are worried about paying extra taxes, look at some of these ideas as ways to shift your tax burden. Once again, don't go crazy. Before you rush off on that junket to Hawaii or Europe, consult with your tax advisor first. Make sure the trip is deductible in your situation.

Two other ideas while we're on the subject of tax deductions. You can use your business income to help fund your retirement or shift money to your kids by employing them to work in your business.

When you own your own business, you can fund a personal retirement account, 401K, SEP IRA, or KEOGH. The individual details are beyond the scope of this book; consult a tax professional for more details.

If you have kids, put them to work for your company and pay them the money you would have given them anyway. If you have college-age kids, this is an excellent way to help them pay for college while deducting the expense from your business. Keep in mind when you do this, it is just like hiring a regular employee. You need to pay unemployment taxes and provide a W-2 at the end of the year.

Choosing Your Business Structure

How you structure your business is crucial to how much money you will keep at the end of the year.

Most eBay businesses will take one of the following structures.

1) Sole proprietorship
2) Partnership
3) Corporation
4) Small business corporation (Subchapter S)

Sole proprietorship

A sole proprietorship is the simplest form of business entity. It is run by one person with no distinction between the individual and the business. If the business makes money, you keep all of the profits. If the business loses money, you are responsible for all the losses.

Most sole proprietorships are conducted using the business owner's name. If you choose to run it under a different name, you may need to file a DBA (Doing Business As). Usually, you would register your business with the City Clerk's Office or a county office and pay a small fee. They will check to see if the name you want to use is already in use. If it is being used by another business, you need to choose another name.

Your business income should be recorded on Schedule C of your IRS 1040 tax form and is taxed at your regular rate.

The major disadvantage of a sole proprietorship is you are 100% responsible for business liabilities. If you sell defective products or someone gets hurt on your business premises, you are fully responsible and can be sued for liability.

Partnership

A partnership is a business relationship between two or more people. Partners typically sign a partnership agreement. Each of them contributes a certain amount of capital and labor and shares in its profits or losses.

Partners can share equally in the profits, or some partners may have a more significant ownership percentage based upon the partnership agreement. Income is reported to each partner on a form called a Schedule K-1.

The disadvantage again is partners are fully responsible for any liabilities contracted by the business.

Corporation

A corporation is an independent legal entity owned by its shareholders. The business is registered with the State Corporation Department or Secretary of State's Office. They are required to have business licenses and permits and to file quarterly and annual reports with the state they are incorporated in.

Corporations are typically owned by many people who are issued shares in exchange for investing capital in the business.

Shareholders in the corporation receive income in the form of dividends. The most significant advantage of a corporation is income is taxed at a lower corporate rate, and liability is limited to the money you have invested in the corporation. If the products you sell injure someone, in most cases, customers cannot come back on you personally.

Subchapter S Corporation

Subchapter S corporations pass earnings and losses through to shareholders for federal tax purposes. Shareholders report income on their personal tax returns and pay taxes at their standard rate.

To qualify as an S Corporation, the corporation must file [Form 2553 Election by a Small Business Corporation](http://www.irs.gov/pub/irs-pdf/f2553.pdf).

S Corporations have many advantages that make them attractive to online business owners.

- Your assets are protected. The most you can lose as an investor is the money you have invested in the corporation.
- You can reduce self-employment tax liability by paying yourself a portion of your income as salary and dividends.
- Corporations have pass-through taxation, which allows owners to report losses or earnings on their personal tax returns.
- It opens up new possibilities in offering yourself corporate perks such as better retirement plans, writing off college expenses, and other benefits. Be sure to consult with a qualified tax advisor before implementing any of these ideas.

The odds are most online businesses will begin life as a sole proprietorship and scale up as the business grows.

Business Permits, Licenses, and Such

Most eBay sellers run their businesses out of their homes. The majority of their neighbors don't know anything about it, except for the frequent comings and goings of the mail trucks, UPS vans, and Fed Ex guys.

As such, most eBay sellers don't bother with licenses or permits. They go about their daily routine pretty much unaware they may be breaking local codes and regulations.

What I'm going to do here is talk about the different licenses and permits a typical eBay business owner might bump up against. Then, I will give you a few tips on how to get them.

DBA (Doing Business As). If you conduct your business using an assumed (fictitious) name, you must record your information with the city clerk's office or county clerk's office, depending upon where you live. Sometimes you can fill out the form online. Other times you will be required to go into the appropriate office and pay a small fee. They check to see if the name is being used by another company in your area. If it is, you will need to pick a new name. Banks will require a copy of your DBA if you attempt to open an account in your business's name.

Business License. Most cities and counties require a license to conduct business within their boundaries. The fees vary based upon the type of business you run. Where I live, you apply for a license with the city's department of revenue. If you are unsure where to apply for a business license in your area Google "city name business license."

EIN (Employer Identification Number). Most online businesses conduct their business using the owner's social security number. If you prefer not to share that information, you can apply to the IRS for an EIN. Here is a link to apply for an EIN online https://www.us-tax-id-number.com/?gclid=CJaB3Kq_jr4CFckWMgod63cAbQ.

Home Business Permit. Some municipalities require homeowners to register if they are conducting a business out of their homes. Call your city clerk's office to learn more about your area's licensing requirements.

Sales & Use Tax Permit. If you make sales to residents of your state, you are required to collect sales tax. Contact your state department of revenue for more information.

  The SBA has an excellent website covering local business licenses that may be required. They even have a search feature where you can enter your zip code, and it will return a list of business licenses and permits you may require. Follow this link for more details

http://www.sba.gov/licenses-and-permits

Sell your Stuff Off eBay

For most sellers, eBay is the place to cut your teeth in online selling. The site is easy to use. They have a built base of nearly 182 million eager buyers, and it's relatively inexpensive to get started.

The big four alternatives to selling on eBay are –

1. Amazon
2. Etsy
3. Fiverr
4. Personal website

Which marketplace is the correct choice for your business depends upon what you sell, your sales volume, and your business goals.

If you sell products, Amazon is the clear choice for where to start selling next. If you sell handmade crafts or crafting supplies, Etsy would be a good choice. If you sell services such as eBook covers, website design, whiteboard videos, etc. Fiverr is a solid choice.

A personal website makes an excellent addition to selling on the above e-commerce sites. As a standalone sales solution—it's not a good choice for most sellers.

The reason is the big e-commerce sites let you tap into their built-in customer base and reach hundreds of millions of ready customers. A personal website is only as strong as your mailing list.

If you're just starting out, that can be as few as ten or twenty customers, maybe even zero.

Amazon is the 800-pound gorilla in the market when it comes to e-commerce.

Amazon and eBay ran neck-and-neck in sales for the year ending 2020. Amazon racked up $125.56 billion in sales; eBay came in at $100 billion (excluding auto sales). Both sites benefited greatly from the pandemic. eBay sales jumped nearly $15 billion, while Amazon rocketed up over $39 billion. Amazon has 310 million registered users worldwide—almost half of them are enrolled in Amazon Prime. eBay has 185 million registered users worldwide.

No other e-commerce sites come close.

If you're considering selling on another e-commerce platform, Amazon should be your first choice.

Fees run about the same on both sites. The difference is eBay sellers pay listing and store fees to place their items on the site. Amazon sellers don't pay any listing or store fees (Amazon does have a Pro Merchant plan for $39.99 per month. It reduces the per-item fee sellers pay when items sell and lets sellers add new items to Amazon's catalog. I'll discuss this in more detail shortly.)

In most cases selling on Amazon is a matter of searching for a product similar to the one you want to sell. After you've located a similar product, select the *Sell on*

Amazon button below the buy box, and follow the prompts. Essential items you need to supply are the condition of the item you wish to sell and the price.

Unlike eBay, there's no need to upload pictures, create product descriptions, or write titles—for most of the items you're going to sell, that information is already in place.

On Amazon, you're basically a hitchhiker on the item listing page.

Each product has one product description page. Buyers click on the price links to the item they're looking at. It brings up a list of sellers who have the product available and the price and condition it is available in.

If you sell one-of-a-kind items not currently listed on Amazon, you can create a new catalog listing for your item. Key points to remember when setting up a new catalog page include –

1. Personal branding is not allowed.
2. Descriptions should be product-focused. Don't talk about your company, service, or selling policies.
3. Include product-related photos only. Don't include any company info in your photos.
4. Select your shipping service and price. Some categories, such as books, require you to select Amazon's shipping services and fees.

5. Set the product condition. If you have multiples of an item in different conditions—list one item. Then add the next one by describing the condition it is in.

Under Amazon's current terms of service, all sellers can set up new catalog pages in most categories. Pro Merchant accounts give you more flexibility.

The fee for a Pro Merchant account is $39.99 per month. If you sell more than forty items per month, it'll save you some money. The reason is Amazon charges a 99¢ per item transaction fee for all items sold—Pro Merchant account holders aren't charged the fee.

When you mention Etsy, what comes to most people's minds is crafts, but it's actually a whole lot more. A quick glance through the site will show you sellers offering to design websites, create blog themes, layout business cards, or draw custom-made artwork.

If you plan to sell on Etsy, you need to understand it's more of a community than eBay or Amazon. Buyers and sellers take time out to socialize and comment on each-others items. You can increase your chances of success by joining in the conversation.

Etsy is more folksy and down to earth. The first thing you notice is the look and feel of their primary sales page. It's more visual than the other e-commerce sites. When you view the category home pages, there are no extra words, pricing, etc.—it's all visual. The entire page is nothing but product images with short descriptions under the pictures like shorts, pants, and prints.

When you click into a category, you're presented with another page of illustrations dished up very similar to how you'd see them on Pinterest. The only text you're shown in this view is the title, the seller's name below it, and the price.

The product description pages are bolder and more visual than those you find on eBay and Amazon.

At the top of the page, there's a large picture of your item. Arrow buttons let you click through the pictures. To the right of the picture, you'll find a product highlights box that includes the title, price, product overview, and a buy button at the bottom where you can add the item to your cart.

Further down the page, there's a more detailed description of the item, where you can tell more about it or how you conceived and created the product. There's a large product gallery on the right side of the page that features some of your other items.

You can add a Meet the Owner section at the bottom of the page that includes a picture to introduce you to buyers.

It's a totally unique shopping experience compared to eBay or Amazon. You need to play to this difference to maximize sales.

Pictures are the key to making more sales. Spend extra time shooting the best pictures you can. Close-up shots work best, especially of intricate design work. When you look at the clothing section, the best illustrations have people modeling the clothes. Some sellers include full-body pictures, including their faces; others choose to cut them off at the neck. Another option would be to use a mannequin.

If you sell smaller items, consider investing in a lightbox. It will help you take better close-up pictures and get the lighting just right. You can find them online starting at thirty dollars.

The best descriptions are short. They should include a lot of white space and bullet points. I notice many sellers give a short description followed by bullet points highlighting their item's key features.

Other descriptions focus on the product. Sellers talk about what inspired their design, how they made it, and the materials used to make it. This is especially true with crafts and art prints. However, I've noticed several sellers use this method to talk about the designs on the clothing they sell.

If you're selling handmade items, crafts, or customized clothing or jewelry, you definitely want to make Etsy one of your seller platforms. If you offer graphic design or website services, you can command a premium price on Etsy. The key to making more sales is to customize your pitch to crafters.

One of my books is called *Etsy Bookkeeping Made Easy*. It's a perfect fit to offer on Etsy. Another one of my books, *Sell it Online*, has a section on Etsy marketing, so I will probably be offering it there soon, too.

For sellers offering crafting guides, patterns, and similar items, Etsy may be the perfect marketplace. They also allow digital downloads so you can enable instant delivery.

Sell it on Fiverr

Fiverr is a hip young website where buyers and sellers meet to exchange cash for services.

If you haven't checked it out yet, give it a look over. It's amazing what some of these folks will do for five bucks.

They have people designing WordPress sites, creating book covers, voice-overs, drawing, cartooning, and creating banner ads. You name it, and someone is offering to do it—for five bucks—maybe.

Fiverr offers this fantastic option that lets sellers bump that initial $5.00 purchase to $50.00, $100.00, or more. It's called Gig Extras, and you're gonna love it.

Let me tell you a little more about how Gig Extras work.

Before you can offer Gig Extras, you must complete ten transactions with excellent feedback. After you do that, you're allowed to offer limited Gig Extras. The next step is to level up and become a Level Two seller. This opens up more selling options and gives you the golden ticket to charge more for Gig Extras.

The final step is to become a Top Rated Seller. These are the guys pulling in $40,000, $50,000, or more a year. The process for becoming a top-rated seller is shrouded in mystery. These guys are voted in by Fiverr's Editors. Once they're in the club, even more, selling options open up to them. They can charge up to $100 for each Gig Extra.

Pretty cool, huh?

Now I'll tell you what a Gig Extra is. It's an option buyers can add to their original purchase to enhance it. For example, I purchase a lot of book covers. The cover design itself is $5.00. Most sellers offer a free image with your purchase, or they offer a Gig Extra for a premium image that will make your cover look even better. They charge $5.00 or $10.00 more for the premium image. If they subscribe to an image service, it costs them 50¢ to $1.00, so that's an extra $4.00 to $9.50 in pure profit.

Another popular Gig Extra is to offer one-day or two-day service instead of the standard five to seven days. Buyers who want their item quicker pay an extra $5.00 to $20.00—all of it is pure-profit to the seller.

Other options are to upgrade to a KDP paperback cover or to order a PDF or PSD file of the cover art. The KDP paperback cover takes a few extra minutes to design but brings the seller an extra $10.00 or $20.00 in revenue. The PDF or PSD files don't cost the seller anything extra. They just send the existing file to the buyer.

Some sellers take a more unique approach to Gig Extras. They hang out a cyber-tip jar and encourage buyers to leave a gratuity if they're happy with the product they received. Smart sellers leave detailed options for their tip jars. Check these out and see what you think.

- For $5.00, I will get a Starbucks coffee to start my day.
- For $20.00, I can pump half a tank of gas in my car.
- For $50.00, I can take the wife and kids out for a nice meal.
- For $100.00, I can invest in some new software to grow my business.

The bigger tips are few and far between, but when you hit one, it's like winning the lotto.

That's the magic of Gig Extras. Most of them cost the seller no additional time or money but allow the seller the chance to significantly boost their income.

Getting started on Fiver

The great thing about Fiverr is if you can imagine something, you can probably sell it there.

If it sounds like something that interests you, I'd suggest spending a few days cruising around the site and exploring some of the stuff being sold on there.

Here is a list of some of the more popular gigs on Fiverr.

- Graphic Design. This includes book covers, business cards, banner advertisements, sales flyers, etc.
- White Board Videos. Most sellers offer a short thirty-second video and charge an extra $5.00 for each additional thirty seconds. Some charge more to add public domain music and images.
- Puppet Messages. Puppets are big on Fiverr. One of Fiverr's highest-rated sellers is Professor Puppet. His videos have been used for internet advertisements, Kick-starter campaigns, and more.
- Jingle Writing and Recording. Is music your talent? Lots of aspiring singers offer to record themselves singing your jingle. For an extra $10.00 to $20.00, they'll help you write it.
- Flyer Monger. Let's say you're like me and don't have any special talent. Many people have completed thousands of gigs doing nothing more than passing out flyers on busy streets, college campuses, and major events.

Hopefully, that's whetted your appetite to learn more about Fiverr.

The opportunity is there. You need to move beyond thinking it's just five bucks. With a bit of ingenuity, a clever gig, and the right attitude—Fiverr allows you to make real money doing what you enjoy.

To get, started visit http://www.fiverr.com/.

Sell it on Your Personal Website

Selling from your own website is the ultimate thrill. You have complete control over design, product offerings, and price. You don't have to pay eBay or Amazon their cut.

A personal website is also one of the toughest sells. Bringing customers to your own website is more painful than pulling teeth.

If you decide you need a website, don't go it alone. Stick with a platform like Shopify, Square, or Big Commerce. They charge a small monthly fee and a per-transaction fee for items sold, but the benefits are worth the extra cost—they're easy to set up and let you tap into their customer base.

Shopify is the hottest online store solution today. They offer three different store options ranging from $29.00 to $299.00 per month plus a small per item transaction fee.

I tried the fourteen-day free trial to set up a sample store. It was easy to set up and use. I had my basic design and first few items posted to it in less than an hour.

You can follow this link for more info on using Shopify http://www.shopify.com/. If you're serious about using Shopify, you may want to check out a new book by Brian Patrick called Selling on Shopify.

Other eBay Alternatives

There are a lot of e-commerce websites catering to small and medium-sized online sellers. Most sellers report mixed results selling on these sites. Often it boils down to the products you sell. If you have an established clientele, you can send them to your storefront.

Four providers I've tried are –

. eCrater. The best thing about eCrater is they make it easy to import your items from eBay. Select <import your eBay products>, enter your eBay user id, and follow the prompts. They can't make it much simpler than that.

The biggest problem I have with eCrater, is they don't synch your inventory. You need to update your other marketplaces manually each time something sells.

As far as sales go, I sell maybe five to ten items a year on eCrater. The traffic just isn't there—not for historical memorabilia anyway.

.bidStart. This is another e-commerce site that makes it extremely simple to import your items from eBay. The other nice thing is bidStart has a service that syncs your inventory between the two sites. As a result, you never have to worry about inventory problems.

I've been selling on bidStart for several years now. Like eCrater, they're a nice site, they're easy to use, but the traffic just isn't there to make it pay off. If I'm lucky, I make two or three sales a year on bidStart.

.eBid. I got started with eBid because, for a while, it was being touted as the next eBay. They ran a special where you could get started selling for $49.00 and not have to worry about more fees—ever. My eBay fees at the time were $1800 to $2000 a month, so no more fees sounded pretty good.

Ten years later, I've made one sale on eBid for $12.99. That's a net loss of $37.00.

One of the problems is they don't have an eBay import tool. They ask you to download a spreadsheet and upload all your info that way. It's totally beyond my technical level or the amount of time I want to spend invest. I don't see them growing or attracting many eBay sellers until they develop an easy-to-use import tool.

.Bonanza. I like the look and feel of Bonanza better than eBay. They have an easy-to-use import tool to bring your listings to the site. Bonanza also has a tool to sync all of your items across platforms.

What I like best about Bonanza is they went a step farther than the other e-commerce sites. They added Amazon into the mix. Sellers with an Amazon Pro Merchant account can import their items from their Amazon store into Bonanza and synch them out to eBay and vice-versa. Their service keeps all your items synched, so when something sells on eBay, it is removed from your Bonanza store.

I'm going to be honest. I've never made many sales on the Bonanza site itself, but since they've added the eBay connectivity feature, my sales have shot up on eBay.

So here's what I'm going to say. Use Bonanza to manage your eBay and Amazon listings. Bonanza is cheap compared to other companies out there that perform the same services.

Export Your Store charges $19.99 per month to move your eBay items to Amazon and keep them synched. Amazon requires sellers to have a Pro Merchant account to access their API, so keep in mind that's another $39.99 per month no matter which service you use.

Bonanza also has an excellent promotional program available to drive Google traffic to your listings. You can choose the percentage of your selling price you want to use for promotional fees—they range from 3.5% to 16%. The choices they offer for advertising your item include broadcasting it to Google Shopping, the Find, eBay, Nextag, and Bing Ads.

Promotion is an essential consideration for eBay sellers now that eBay has cheaped out and stopped purchasing Google AdWords for their listings. It may even be more critical now since eBay was penalized by Google for Black Hat SEO tactics. Since early 2014 nearly fifty percent of eBay's listings have been penalized and removed from Google search.

www.ingramcontent.com/pod-product-compliance
Lightning Source LLC
Chambersburg PA
CBHW031426210526
45464CB00005B/2078